HELICOPTERS

IAN GRAHAM

Designed and produced by
Aladdin Books Ltd
70 Old Compton Street
London W1

*First published in the
United States in 1989 by*
Gloucester Press
387 Park Avenue South
New York, NY 10016

ISBN 0-531-17171-X

Library of Congress Catalog
Card Number: 88-50452

Design David West
Children's Book Design

Editorial Lionheart Books

Research Cecilia Weston-Baker

Illustrators Aziz Khan
Ron Hayward Associates

Printed in Belgium

CONTENTS

HOW · IT · WORKS
HELICOPTERS

IAN GRAHAM

GLOUCESTER PRESS

New York · London · Toronto · Sydney

THE WORKING PARTS

A helicopter is an aircraft that can fly in any direction and hover in mid-air. Instead of fixed wings, it has a moving wing called a rotor that acts as a wing and a propeller.

The main working part of a helicopter is the rotor head. This is a complicated set of metal rods, hinges and plates that connects the engines and the pilot's controls to the rotor blades. The rotor head is spun at high speed by the engines. As the blades attached to it cut through the air, they behave like long thin wings. This produces a force called

Swept blade tip fairing

Rotor head

Turboshaft engine

Pilot's seat

Collective pitch control

Gunner/copilot seat

Targeting unit

Gun barrel

Avionics unit
Engine power levers

Main undercarriage

Antitank missiles

lift that raises the helicopter straight up into the air. A second, smaller rotor on the tail stops the helicopter itself from spinning. The pilot can move the helicopter in different directions by pushing on a control stick in the cockpit. This changes the tilt, or angle, of the rotor head or blades.

The cockpit of each helicopter is positioned in front of the engines. It has large windows to give the pilot a clear view ahead and around the aircraft. The main engine drive-rod, or shaft, runs along the body, or fuselage of the helicopter to the tail section.

Tailplane

Tail rotor

Rotor blade

Gearbox

Rear wheel

Tail rotor transmission shaft

McDonnell Douglas AH-64 Apache

Exhaust duct

Turboshaft engine

Helicopters are useful vehicles as they can take off and land in areas too small for ordinary aircraft. The type of things a helicopter must carry – cargo, weapons, people or a combination of these – and the conditions in which it has to work determine its size, shape and rotor design.

DIFFERENT KINDS

There are different types of helicopters for different kinds of work. Military attack helicopters like the Bell Huey Cobra are small, lightweight, yet robust, and agile so they can fly fast, maneuver well and carry many weapons.

Transport helicopters, for example the twin-rotor Boeing Chinook, are big enough to carry cargo or passengers inside. Alternatively, heavy loads, for instance road vehicles, may be hung underneath the helicopter. Transport helicopters are fitted with very powerful engines to cope with the large loads they have to lift.

Helicopters are also used to rescue people after accidents at sea and transport them back to land. The Sikorsky Sea King is a typical rescue helicopter, yet it can do many other kinds of jobs too. It was designed as a military helicopter to hunt for enemy submarines, but today it is also used for passenger and cargo transport, air-sea rescue and troop-carrying.

Such general purpose helicopters must be large enough to carry people inside and powerful enough to lift heavy loads. Their engines must also use up fuel slowly so that they can hover over one place for long periods. Some of these helicopters are often built in two different versions – one for military operations and one for civilian use.

The American AH-64 Apache attack helicopter

A Sea King on rescue work

Powerful helicopters transport heavy loads

A city-center commuter helicopter

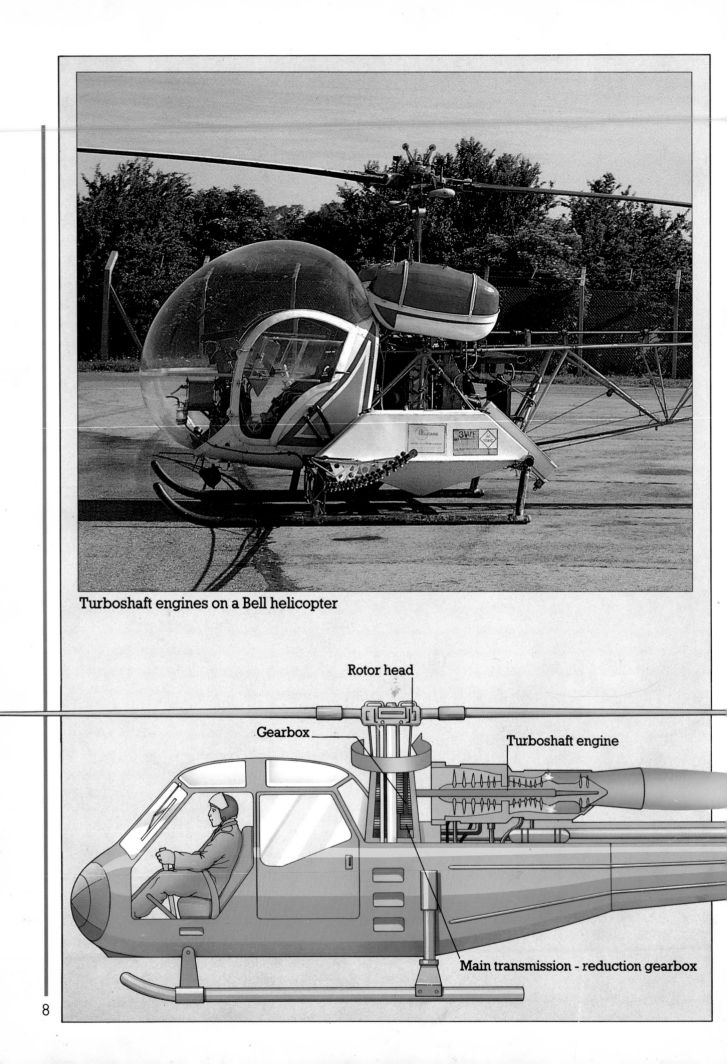

Turboshaft engines on a Bell helicopter

Rotor head

Gearbox

Turboshaft engine

Main transmission - reduction gearbox

CREATING THE POWER

The earliest helicopters, built in the 1930s and 1940s, were powered by gasoline-fueled engines similar to car engines. In the 1950s, a new type of engine called a turboshaft was developed for helicopters. It produced more power than a gas engine of the same size, and used kerosene fuel, which is less expensive and less flammable than gasoline. The Alouette, made in France in 1955, was one of the first helicopters to use such an engine.

Today, helicopters still use turboshaft engines. All but the smallest helicopters are fitted with two engines. This is for two important reasons. Firstly, two small engines can create more power than a single large engine. Secondly, two engines are safer than one in the event of a failure. If one engine fails and loses power, the remaining engine enables the pilot to make a controlled landing.

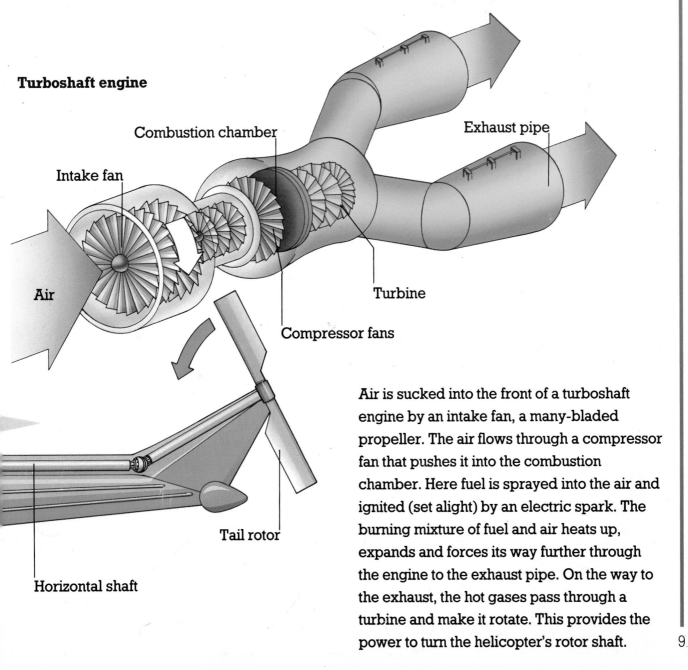

Turboshaft engine

Combustion chamber

Exhaust pipe

Intake fan

Air

Turbine

Compressor fans

Tail rotor

Horizontal shaft

Air is sucked into the front of a turboshaft engine by an intake fan, a many-bladed propeller. The air flows through a compressor fan that pushes it into the combustion chamber. Here fuel is sprayed into the air and ignited (set alight) by an electric spark. The burning mixture of fuel and air heats up, expands and forces its way further through the engine to the exhaust pipe. On the way to the exhaust, the hot gases pass through a turbine and make it rotate. This provides the power to turn the helicopter's rotor shaft.

TAKING OFF

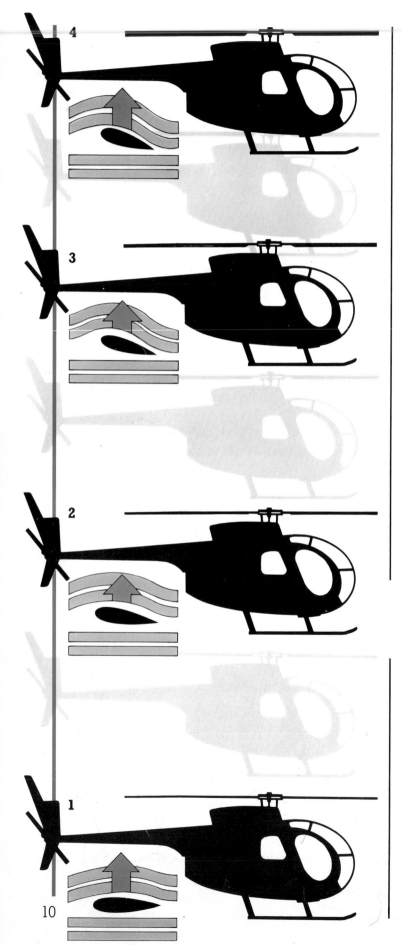

When the pilot starts the helicopter engine, the rotor blades begin to rotate, slowly at first. (The circle that the tips of the blades trace out in the air as they spin is called the rotor disc.)

When the engine runs up to flight speed and the blades are spinning quickly enough, the pilot raises the collective pitch control lever at his or her side to make all the rotor blades gradually twist by the same amount. They now behave more like aircraft wings and begin to create lift. The lifting force from the blades increases and eventually it overcomes the great weight of the helicopter, which begins to rise straight up into the air.

Helicopters normally take off pointing into the wind for extra lift. If it is necessary to turn the helicopter into the wind, this is done by means of two foot pedals. They control the amount of thrust (pushing force) produced by the small tail rotor. Varying this thrust makes the helicopter spin one way or the other.

Helicopter blades begin spinning parallel to the ground (1) producing very little lift. When the pilot operates the collective pitch control, the leading edge of each blade rises. Air flowing over the top of the blade travels faster than the air slipping beneath it. This reduces the air pressure above the blade and creates suction that produces lift (2). Twisting the blades more produces even greater lift (3) and the helicopter rises. Boosting engine speed using the collective lever twist-grip also increases lift (4).

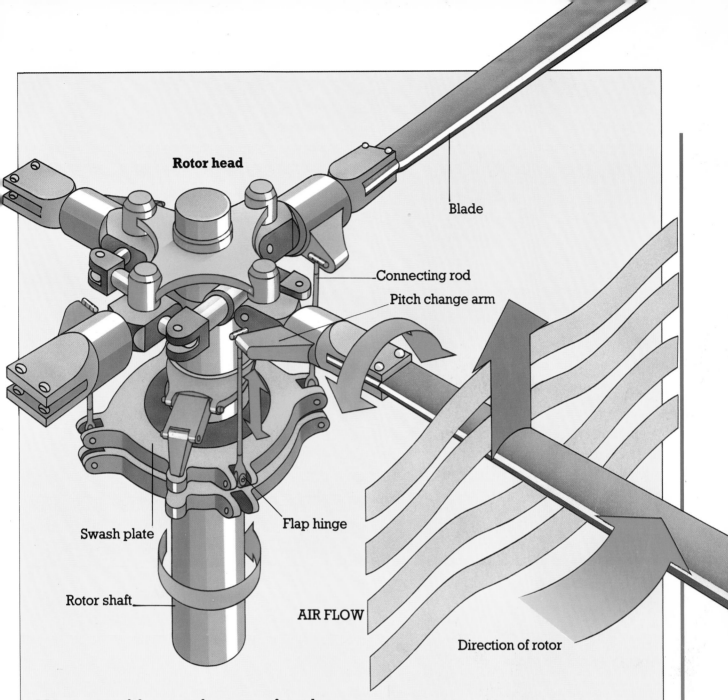

Rotor head

Blade

Connecting rod

Pitch change arm

Flap hinge

Swash plate

Rotor shaft

AIR FLOW

Direction of rotor

Movements of the controls are transferred
to the blades by the swash plate. This
consists of two halves. The upper part spins
with the rotor head while the lower part
stays still. A bearing between the two
transfers the pilot's commands from the
lower to the upper half. If the whole plate
rises, all the blades are twisted by the same
amount and lift increases evenly all around
the rotor disc. If the swash plate tilts, the
blades are angled up when they pass over
the high side of the plate and down at the
opposite side. Extra lift is produced in only
one part of the rotor disc.

A Bell 206B set Ranger 2 taking off.

HOVERING

One of the major advantages that helicopters have over all fixed-wing aircraft is that they can hang motionless in the air. This is called hovering.

Airplane wings can only produce enough lift to support the aircraft's weight when the craft is traveling forward at great speed. A helicopter's rotor blades can produce lift even when the helicopter is stationary. This is because the blades themselves are driven around very rapidly.

To hover, the pilot holds the cyclic control stick in a central position to keep the rotor disc level. Any forces from crosswinds that try to push the helicopter sideways can be overcome by tilting the rotor disc to produce a force in the opposite direction.

Hovering is useful for several jobs that helicopters do. An air-sea rescue helicopter can hover over a ship in difficulty while the crew is lifted off the deck one or two people at at time. A mountain rescue helicopter can hover just above rough ground that no other vehicle could reach while an injured mountaineer is placed on board.

The force that spins a helicopter's blades in one direction could also spin the rest of the helicopter in the opposite direction.

A small rotor at the end of the helicopter's tail provides a sideways force to prevent the helicopter itself from spinning.

Without tail rotor – helicopter spins and wobbles

With tail rotor – helicopter stable

A Sea King hovers over the sea and dips a submarine sensor under the water.

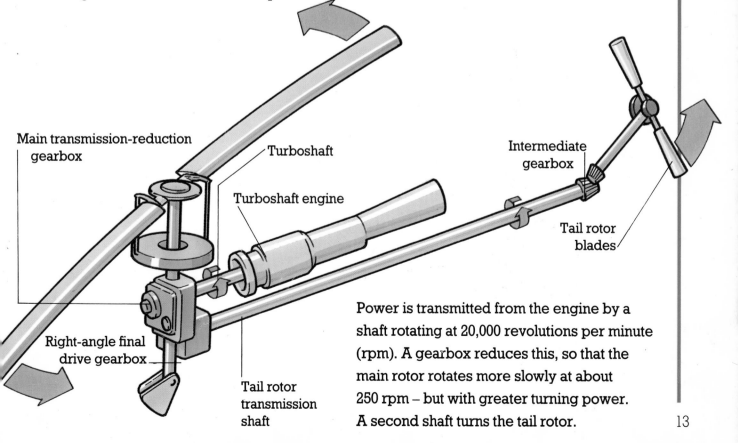

Main transmission-reduction gearbox

Turboshaft

Turboshaft engine

Intermediate gearbox

Tail rotor blades

Right-angle final drive gearbox

Tail rotor transmission shaft

Power is transmitted from the engine by a shaft rotating at 20,000 revolutions per minute (rpm). A gearbox reduces this, so that the main rotor rotates more slowly at about 250 rpm – but with greater turning power. A second shaft turns the tail rotor.

The Bell 222 helicopter

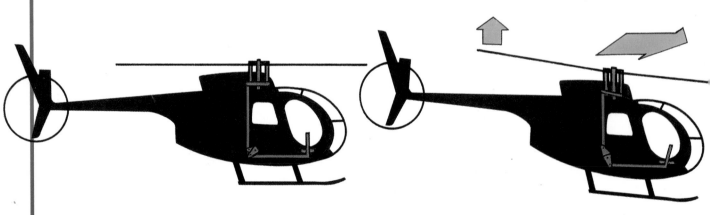

1

With the cyclic control stick in a central position, the rotor disc is level (horizontal) and lift is straight up.

2

When the cyclic control stick is pushed forwards, the whole rotor disc tips forward.

GOING FORWARDS

As a helicopter in the air picks up speed, more lift is created on one side of the craft than on the other. If the rotor blades were rigid, the helicopter would lean toward the side supported by less lift and tilt the rotor disc to one side. This would make the helicopter veer to the side away from its straight-line course. To prevent this, flap hinges are built into the blades (see page 11). These allow the blades to bend up and down and absorb any changes in lift as they rotate.

A helicopter's flying speed is limited to about 400 km/h (240mph) because at this speed the tip of each blade flying into the wind approaches the speed of sound. At this speed, the air flow over the blade begins to break up and it loses lift. To increase lift again, the pilot must increase the tilt of all the blades. But as the blades move toward the helicopter's tail, the tilt is too great to produce lift in the slower airstream. Once again, lift is lost.

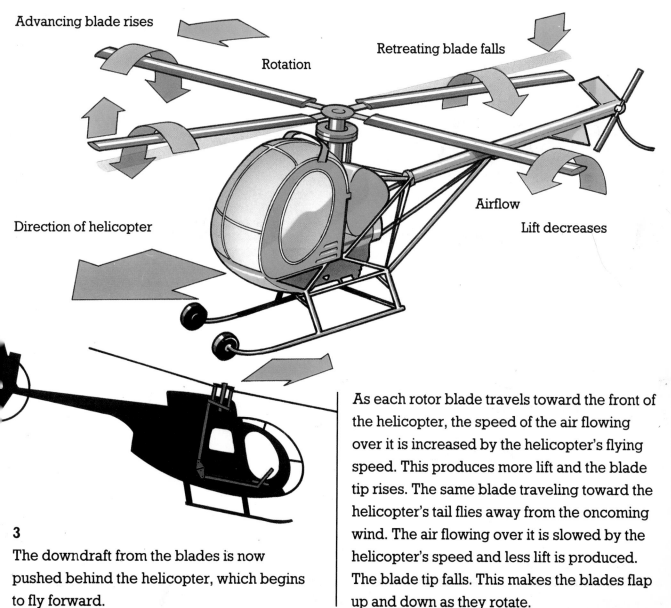

Advancing blade rises

Rotation

Retreating blade falls

Direction of helicopter

Airflow

Lift decreases

3
The downdraft from the blades is now pushed behind the helicopter, which begins to fly forward.

As each rotor blade travels toward the front of the helicopter, the speed of the air flowing over it is increased by the helicopter's flying speed. This produces more lift and the blade tip rises. The same blade traveling toward the helicopter's tail flies away from the oncoming wind. The air flowing over it is slowed by the helicopter's speed and less lift is produced. The blade tip falls. This makes the blades flap up and down as they rotate.

MANEUVERS

A helicopter is a very agile aircraft. The ability to tilt its rotor disc means that the power of its engines can be applied in any direction. The helicopter can therefore fly up or down, sideways, forwards, even backwards, in a very controlled way. This ability is used for hovering and for maneuvering on to landing areas in difficult locations such as a clearing in a forest, a mountain top or the deck of a ship at sea.

Small combat, scout, and observation helicopters, for example the Hughes 500-MD, are highly maneuverable. They can fly fast and very low, hugging the ground contours, which makes them difficult to locate and attack. For these reasons, the helicopter has become important in modern warfare. It can observe the enemy and guide other aircraft in for an attack. In future, the fastest and most agile helicopters may be used to hunt and attack the enemy's helicopter forces.

Blade tilts

When the swash plate tilts, connecting rods transfer the tilt into a twisting motion of the blades. As each blade rotates, a flapping hinge allows it to rise and fall. A drag hinge also allows small forward and backward movements.

Blade also drags back

Blade connecting rod

Rotor shaft

Lower swash plate

Blade

Upper swash plate

Maneuvering a helicopter involves tilting the rotor disc to point the downdraft of air from the rotors in different directions.

To fly to one side, the pilot pushes the cyclic control stick to that side. The swash plate is tilted slightly to create the desired flight.

Some helicopters have rotor blades without hinges. Instead, each blade has a flexible section where it joins the rotor hub. It twists like a hinged blade but in a much more controllable way. This allows helicopters like the Lynx and Apache to fly in ways that other helicopters cannot. They can roll, loop-the-loop or fly upside down. If a helicopter with normal blades tried such maneuvers, the force of the air against the rotor unit would snap the blades or cause the connecting rods to fracture.

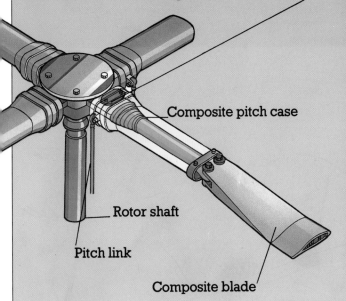

Flexible and elastic damper and beam section

Composite pitch case

Rotor shaft

Pitch link

Composite blade

A Lynx helicopter makes a nose-dive

To fly backward, the pilot pulls back the cyclic control stick. This makes the rotor disc tilt backward. The helicopter's tail drops and its nose comes up. The downdraft from the blades is now directed forward and the lift rearward.

LANDING

Although helicopters can be made to hover and to move up and down in the air while staying level, they are rarely landed vertically. A pilot bringing his or her helicopter straight down to the ground cannot see directly underneath the craft. So unless the helicopter is continually rotated on the way down, the pilot cannot ensure that its tail will not be struck by an object. Closer to the ground, the effect of the helicopter's downdraft rocks the aircraft about.

To overcome these flight problems helicopters are usually made to descend at an angle called the glide-slope. If the helicopter is to land at an airport, the pilot may use an Instrument Landing System (ILS). Radio beams transmitted from the ground are received by the helicopter and are used to show the helicopter's position relative to the glide-slope on an ILS instrument in front of the pilot. To make the helicopter lose height, the pilot lowers the collective pitch lever to lower the angle of the rotor blades.

Decreasing height at a 40°-60° angle

Decreasing height on its own slipstream

If a helicopter tries to land vertically, the downdraft from its rotor blades disturbs the airflow underneath the helicopter. This so-called turbulence makes the helicopter wobble about. To avoid the effects of turbulence, helicopters are normally brought in to land at an angle.

Helicopters can carry passengers into city centers where other aircraft cannot operate.

Helicopters are used to ferry oil workers between offshore oil rigs and land bases.

CONTROLS

A helicopter is not an easy aircraft to fly. The pilot needs to use both hands and both feet to operate the flight controls. Tiny adjustments must be made to the controls all the time to keep the helicopter stable and flying in the desired way. In addition, the pilot must operate navigation and communications equipment and, in a military helicopter, weapons systems too.

When any one of the controls is operated, its effect on the helicopter is shown on an array of instruments on a panel in front of the pilot. The pilot has to watch these instruments as well as look out through the windshield. In a helicopter with a crew of two, some of the instruments are fitted to both sides of the panel so that the pilot and the copilot can each check the craft's workings. Control levers and pedals may also be fitted to both sides of the cockpit, so that the copilot can take over flight control in an emergency.

The control panel of a Dauphin II

The cyclic control stick in front of the pilot controls the direction in which the helicopter flies. Raising and lowering the collective pitch control lever at the pilot's left side varies the amount of lift from the main rotor. Turning a twist grip on this lever controls the engine speed. The pilot can also use foot pedals to alter the thrust from the tail rotor and turn the helicopter to point in different directions.

Cyclic control stick

Throttle

Directional control pedals

Collective pitch control lever

Cyclic control stick to take helicopter backward, forward and side to side

Collective pitch lever to raise or lower helicopter

Directional control pedals to turn left or right while hovering

EMERGENCY

If a helicopter has an engine failure or any other fault that cuts off power to the main rotor, it does not simply fall out of the sky. The unpowered rotor slows down and loses lift. As the helicopter begins to lose height, the direction of the air flowing through the main rotor is reversed, from downward to upward. This creates some lift.

The pilot must always keep the freewheeling rotor spinning as its wing-like effect will be needed later if power cannot be restored. This is done by changing the pitch (angle) of the blades. If engine power is lost while the helicopter is flying slowly or hovering, the pilot may deliberately tip the helicopter's nose downward in order to increase its airspeed and keep the rotor turning as fast as possible.

As the helicopter rushes down toward the ground, the blade angle is altered once more to provide enough lift to soften the landing. All except the smallest helicopters, and especially those that are intended to operate over the sea, have two engines to provide an extra margin of safety.

When a helicopter loses power and therefore lift (1), the pilot first lowers the collective pitch lever to keep the rotor turning. When the craft is close to the ground, this lever is raised so that the rotor provides enough lift to slow the rate of descent (2), then make a controlled approach (3) and a safe landing (4).

A helicopter ditches into the sea in an emergency.

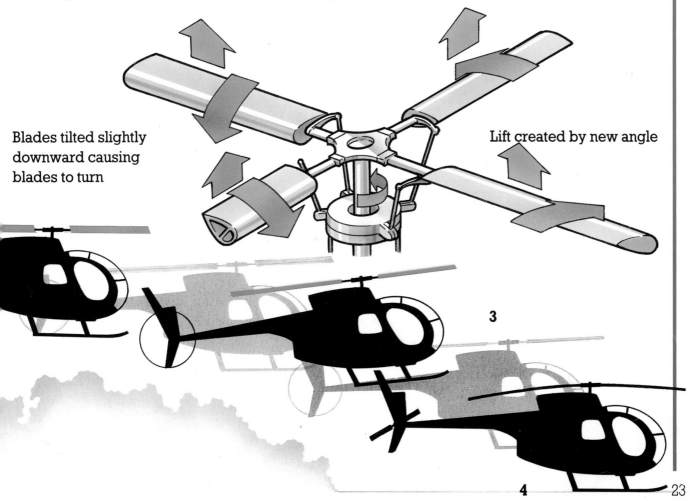

Blades tilted slightly downward causing blades to turn

Lift created by new angle

3

4

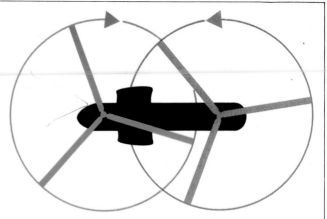

A Boeing twin-rotor helicopter

The Chinook, made by the American company Boeing Vertol, has two main rotors, one at each end of the aircraft. It is used to carry troops, military vehicles and artillery. It is also powerful enough to transport other (damaged) helicopters to base for repair.

A Kamov Ka-22 with "tandem" rotors

Sikorsky's Advancing Blade Concept (ABC) helicopter has two rotors, one above the other on the same rotor head. They spin in opposite directions. At high flying speeds, the loss of lift on one side of one rotor is balanced by the extra lift on that side from the second rotor.

ROTARY VARIATIONS

Most helicopters have a large overhead rotor driven by one or two engines, with a small rotor at the end of a long tail. The tail rotor uses fuel and engine power, but it does not help to lift the helicopter.

Some helicopters do not have a tail rotor, but have two main overhead rotors spinning in opposite directions. The turning force on the helicopter produced by each rotor is canceled out by the other. This has the same effect as the tail rotor. It prevents the helicopter from spinning in the opposite direction

to the main rotor.

Another type of aircraft, called an autogyro, looks like a helicopter but works in a different way. An autogyro's overhead rotor is not driven by an engine. It freewheels. To get airborne, the autogyro is first driven forward by a small back rotor. Air blows upward through the main rotor and starts it spinning. The spinning blades produce lift, as in a helicopter, and the autogyro takes off. Autogyros can land vertically but they cannot hover in the air.

An autogyro produces lift from a freewheeling main rotor.

An autogyro on its takeoff run. The blade tips bend and spread lift over the rotor. Air blows upward through the unpowered overhead rotor and produces enough lift for takeoff.

Main rotor turns, creating lift

Height increases

Autogyro driven forward by back rotor

25

SPECIAL HELICOPTERS

New kinds of aircraft are being developed all the time as designers search for ways of combining the best features of helicopters and airplanes. Helicopters can take off vertically, but they cannot fly faster than 400 km/h (240 mph). Fixed-wing aircraft can fly at over 2,000 km/h (1,200 mph) but, apart from the Harrier "Jump-jet," they cannot take off vertically.

The tilt-rotor combines the two by having engines that rotate from horizontal to vertical. The first tilt-rotor aircraft will enter service with the U.S. military in the 1990s. It will be able to take off vertically and fly at up to 560 km/h (335 mph). An X-Wing looks like a helicopter, but its four broad, stiff rotors behave more like wings. The X-Wing will take longer to develop.

The X-Wing is an advanced aircraft being developed by Sikorsky in the U.S.A.

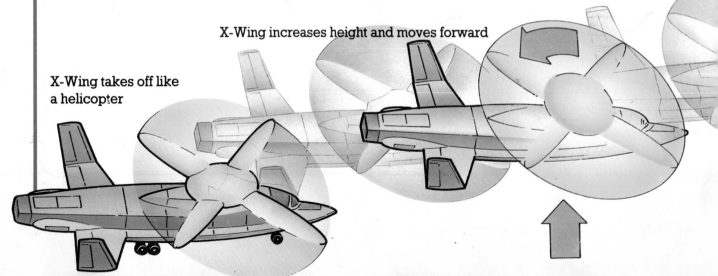

X-Wing increases height and moves forward

X-Wing takes off like a helicopter

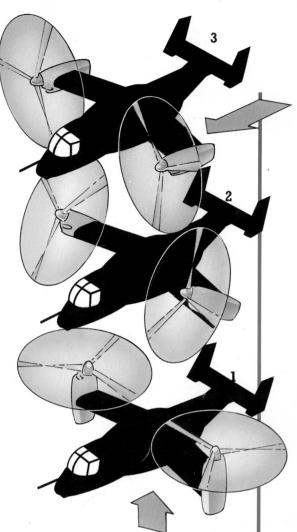

The V-22 Osprey tilt-rotor aircraft

The Osprey tilt-rotor craft takes off vertically by using its two rotors (1). The blades can be twisted to vary the amount of lift they produce. When the Osprey is airborne, its engines are tilted forward slowly (2) until all their thrust is directed backward (3). The Osprey then flies forward like an airplane, with its wings providing all the necessary lift. To land, the Osprey's engines and their rotors tilt back to the vertical.

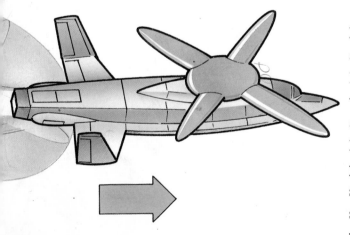

When X-Wing reaches speed, the rotor is turned off

X-Wing is a new type of aircraft that is neither a helicopter nor an airplane. It takes off like a helicopter by rotating its four wings. The wings cannot be twisted like helicopter rotors, and as the rotor disc cannot be tilted, the X-Wing must use the thrust of a jet or propeller for forward flight. When the flying speed is high enough, the wings stop spinning. From then on they behave like fixed wings, and the aircraft can increase speed up to about 850 km/h (510 mph).

HISTORY OF HELICOPTERS

Detailed drawings of a helicopter-like flying machine were made as long ago as the 15th century by the Italian painter and engineer Leonardo da Vinci. Leonardo's design used a device called an airscrew to provide lift instead of the rotor blades that modern helicopters use. It is not known if Leonardo's helicopter was ever built, but it would not have lifted far off the ground.

Leonardo's drawing for a helicopter

The first helicopters were built in the early years of the 20th century. In 1907, four years after the Wright brothers made the first flight in a heavier-than-air machine, a man was lifted into the air by the first helicopter. It was the Breguet-Richet Gyroplane No.1. It was very unstable and had to be kept steady by four people holding onto ropes.

The modern helicopter took shape in the 1930s. The Breguet-Dorand 314 (1936) was the first helicopter to use collective and cyclic pitch control. In 1939, the Ukranian-born American, Igor Sikorsky, demonstrated a helicopter with a single main rotor and a smaller tail rotor, the arrangement still used by most helicopters today.

Early Sikorsky V3-300 (1939)

Few helicopters were built or used during World War II. The development of a new type of engine, called a turboshaft, enabled extremely rapid advancements to be made in all helicopters in the 1950s. During the Korean War (1950-53) helicopters were used to pick up wounded soldiers and aircrew trapped in enemy-held land. During the Vietnam War in the 1960s and 1970s helicopters were used extensively for this and other jobs. Bell "Huey" and Chinook helicopters ferried troops into and out of battle, and the world's first attack helicopter, the Huey Cobra "gunship," went into service. The Huey's nickname came from its original 1955 model name, the HU-1A.

A Bell Huey in use in Vietnam

During the Vietnam War the helicopter was used to attack tanks for the first time and it is now a very effective antitank weapon. Its success led to the design of other fast, very maneuverable combat helicopters, like the Hughes AH-64 Apache and the Soviet Mil MI-24 "Hind."

The importance of the submarine in modern warfare has also led to the development of anti-sub helicopters, for example the Sea King. These are equipped with sonar detectors.

A Hughes AH-64 Apache

Helicopters have become such effective combat machines that it will be important to destroy them in future wars. The best weapon to use against a helicopter is another helicopter, a small, fast and very agile anti-helicopter helicopter.

Passenger-carrying helicopters will continue to serve on the shorter air routes, especially to small city center landing pads, called heliports, that airplanes cannot use. Civilian tilt-rotor craft will also begin to operate during the 1990s, probably first in air-sea rescue and coastguard duties, then with passenger services.

FACTS AND FIGURES

The heaviest load ever lifted by a helicopter was carried by a Soviet Mil MI-26 "Halo" in 1982. Its eight-bladed main rotor powered by two 11,000 horse power engines enabled it to lift a total of 56.77 metric tonnes to a height of 2,000 m (6,600 ft).

The world's largest helicopter is a Soviet Mil MI-12 "Homer," also known as a V-12. It has a span across its two rotors of 67 m (220 ft), it is 37 m (121 ft) in length and weighs 114 tons.

The world helicopter speed record is held by a modified Westland Lynx. Its specially shaped rotor blades enabled it to achieve a speed of 400.87 km/h (248.5 mph) in August 1986.

The highest a helicopter has ever flown is 12.44 km (7.69 mi). An SA-315B Lama built by the French company Aérospatiale achieved this record over France in 1972.

The first helicopter pilot's license was issued to British Wing Commander Reginald Brie, the former chief test pilot of the Cierva Autogiro Company in 1947.

The world's first heliport opened at Pier 41 in New York City on May 23, 1949.

The first successful autogyro flight was made by the Spanish engineer Juan de la Cierva, on January 9, 1923, with his model C.4 craft. This consisted of a rotor mounted on the fuselage of a single-engine aircraft.

GLOSSARY

airfoil
A surface such as an aircraft wing that is shaped to produce lift.

altimeter
An instrument for measuring and displaying the height of an aircraft.

autogyro
An aircraft that uses a freewheeling overhead rotor to generate lift when the craft is driven forward by a powered rotor.

bird
Slang term for a helicopter.

chopper
Like "bird," this is a slang term for a helicopter.

cockpit
The part of a helicopter where the pilot sits and controls the aircraft.

collective
A control used to alter the angle of all the rotor blades.

combustion chamber
The part of an engine where the fuel is mixed with air and burned.

cyclic
Control used to change the helicopter's direction.

drag
A force that resists an object's movement and tries to slow it down.

gearbox
A number of interconnecting toothed wheels used to change the speed and turning power of a rotating shaft.

payload
The cargo, passengers, weapons or any other extra weight carried by a helicopter.

pitch
A front-up/front-down motion of the rotor or helicopter.

reduction gearbox
A gearbox used to reduce the speed (and increase the turning power) of a rotating shaft.

roll
Toppling over to one side or the other.

rotor
A set of blades rotating around a central hub.

rotor blade
One of a number of long, usually flexible, wing-like structures that make up a rotor.

rotor disc
An imaginary disc formed by a helicopter's spinning rotor blades.

swash plate
A device for transferring movements of the cyclic and collective controls in the cockpit to changes in the angle of a helicopter's rotor blades.

throttle

A control used to vary the amount of fuel fed to an engine. Opening the throttle increases the engine speed.

thrust

The pushing force of an engine or the propeller or rotor that it drives.

tilt-rotor

A new type of aircraft that can tilt its whole engine-rotor assembly to provide vertical lift or horizontal thrust.

turbine

A many-bladed propeller inside an aircraft engine, rotated by a stream of air or hot gases from a combustion chamber.

turbulence

Instability in an airstream that prevents the air from flowing smoothly over a wing or rotor blade.

winchman

A helicopter crewman responsible for operating the aircraft's winch, which is a powered pulley system.

X-wing

A new type of aircraft that uses four broad, stiff wings for vertical flight like a helicopter, but which can also stop the wings rotating and fly forward like a fixed-wing airplane.

yaw

A turning motion to the left or right, like a car turning around a corner.

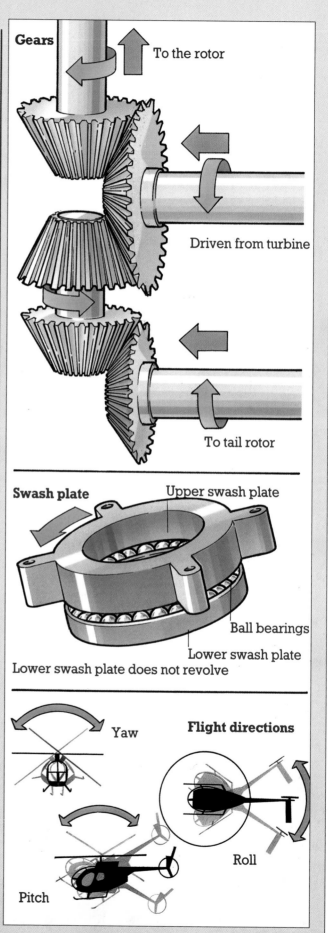

Gears
To the rotor
Driven from turbine
To tail rotor

Swash plate
Upper swash plate
Ball bearings
Lower swash plate
Lower swash plate does not revolve

Yaw
Flight directions
Roll
Pitch

INDEX

Photographic credits
Cover and pages 6, 7bl, 8, 14, 20, 24t, 27 and
29: The Aviation Picture Library; pages 7t, 13,
17 and 28t: Salamander Picture Library; pages
7br, 11, 19 both and 24b: J. Allan Cash; pages
23 and 25: Rex Features; pages 26: NASA.